Weather Folk-Lore Of The Sea

And

Superstitions Of The Scottish Fishermen

WEATHER FOLK-LORE OF THE SEA.

THE following folk-lore on the weather has been collected for the most part from the fisher-folks along the north-east of Scotland. The village or villages in which the observation has been met with are recorded. Reference has been made to two works on folk weather-lore—viz., *Signal Service Notes*, No. ix; *Weather Proverbs*—prepared under the direction of Brigadier and Brevet Major-General W. B. Hazen, Chief Signal Officer of the Army, by H. H. C. Dunwoody, First Lieutenant, 4th Artillery, A. S. O. and Asst., quoted as *D.*, and *On the Popular Weather Prognostics of Scotland*, by Arthur Mitchell, A.M., M.D., member of Council of the Meteorological Society, etc., quoted as *M.*

I.—THE SUN.

A " low dawn"—*i.e.*, when the rays of the sun, before the sun comes above the horizon, illuminate the clouds only a little above the horizon—indicates foul weather (Pittulie). On the other hand, " a high dawn" indicates a fair day.[1]

Daybreak is called " sky-casting" or " sky-making". If the " sky cast" pretty far towards the south, the day is not to be depended on (Pittulie); if well to the east, it is to be depended on.

When the sun rises " fiery" it is a sign of drought, when "white", "sick", or "sickly",of rain[2] (Pittulie,[3] Macduff, Rose-hearty).

When it rises " white and sick", both wind and wet

---

[1] *D.*, p. 78, under " Low and High Dawn".
[2] *Ibid.*, p. 78, under " Pale Sunrise".   [3] *D.*, p. 78.

follow, with the wind from the south or south-west (Rose-hearty).

If the sun rises with a glaring, glassy sort of light accompanied with small glittering clouds, stormy weather is looked for that day.

If after the sun has risen for an hour and a half or two hours his rays appear to shoot down to the horizon, the wind in a short time blows from east by south or south-south-east. Such rays go by the name of "back-stays" (Findochty). In Macduff they are called "staanarts".

When the sun rises "red as blood" a gale is at hand, mostly from the south[1] (Rosehearty). When it appears red, but not very red, about "man-heicht" above the horizon, a fine day follows, with the wind from the south or south-west (Rosehearty).

If the sun comes up unclouded, shines brightly for a time, and then becomes hid by clouds, a common remark is, "He's p——, an gane t' bed". Such a thing is an indication of dull cloudy weather[2] (Pennan).

When the sun appears "sick and foul", that is, when the sun is covered with a grey or "aisy" (ashy) haze, rain follows in summer, and snow in winter (Rosehearty).

In rainy weather, if the sun sets behind heavy black clouds with "clear holes" in them, "roving", *i.e.*, unsettled, weather follows with the wind westerly.[3]

A black cloud rising in the west towards sunset is called "a growan-up", and is a precursor of a near burst of stormy weather (Pittulie).

A large black heavy cloud in the west when the sun is not far from the horizon is called "a bank", and is the forerunner of a strong breeze from the west. The following are the formulæ :—

> "When the sin sets in a clear,
> Wasterly win' ye needna fear ;

---

[1] *D.*, p. 78.   [2] *D.*, p. 79, under "Sunrise".
[3] *D.*, p. 76, under "Cloudy Sunset and Dark Clouds".

> When the sin sets in a bank
> Wasterly win' ye winna want." (Buckie.)

"If the sin set in a bank,
A westerly ween ye winna want ;
If she set clear
An easterly ween is near." (Macduff.)

A variant of the last line is :— '

"An easterly ween will seen be here." (Pennan.)

"Fin the sin sets in a clear,
A wasterly win' ye needna fear ;
Fin the sin sets in a bank
A wasterly win' ye winna want." (Crovie.)

"A clear in the nor' never hairm nae man," said a Portessie man. It is a common opinion that all the bad weather "makes up" in the south-west (Portessie).

"When it thickens in the wast," said a man of Portessie, "it will be southerly winds in the firth."

Of a summer afternoon the rays of the sun stretch at times down to the horizon. The sun is then said to be "shaftit", and there is a formula :—

"A shaftit sin
That's the sign o' a staanin win'." (Crovie.)

Of a summer afternoon, when the sun is westering, there is at times a peculiar glassy-like glitter on the sea. Some fishermen say that it is an indication of coming stormy weather or of rain (Pittulie).

A halo[1] round the sun is called "a sin-bow", and is regarded as the forerunner of rain. The opening in the halo indicates the point from which the wind is to blow (Pittulie). It indicates foul weather (Rosehearty).

A mock-sun goes by the names of :—Dog (general), falcon (Buckie, Portessie), ferrick (general), sin-ferrick, sin-dog (general). The fishermen of Buckie speak of a

---

[1] *D.*, p. 77, under "Halo".

"falcon" hunting the sun, and say that it indicates stormy weather. The following rhymes give the folk-notion of its appearance and position with regard to the weather[1]:—

> " A sin before,
>   The gale is o'er ;
>   A sin behind,
>   The gale ye'll quickly find."   (Buckie.)

> " A sin afore
>   Ye see no more ;
>   A sin ahin'
>   Ye'll shortly fin'."   (Crovie.)

> " A sin before
>   You'll find no more ;
>   A sin behind
>   You're sure to find."   (Port Errol.)

> " One behind
>   You soon shall find ;
>   One before
>   You see no more."

> " A dog afore
>   I'll gar you snore ;
>   A dog ahin'
>   I'll gar you fin'."   (Rosehearty.)

At times the order is reversed :—

> " A sin behind
>   Ye soon shall find ;
>   A sin before
>   Ye get no more."   (Macduff.)

> " A sin behind
>   Ye soon shall find ;
>   A sin before
>   Ye shall no more."   (Footdee.)

---

[1] *D.*, p. 79, under " Sun-dogs". *M.*, p. 16 (7).

> " A ferrick a-wast the sin,
> A sin a-wast the sea ;
> A'll clivv heuks t' nae man,
> An nae man 'ill clivv heuks t' me."

Inland, about Ordiquhill, among old folks the rhyme was :—

> " A ferrick afore,
> Ayont the score ;
> A ferrick ahin'
> Ye'll shortly fin'."

II.—The Moon.

> " A Saiterday's meen
> An a Sunday's fill (same moon),
> Is never good,
> Nor never will."[1] (Pittulie.)

If the new moon is seen shortly after her incoming, un-settled weather is looked for (general).

The new moon lying on her back,[2] and having the points small, is looked upon as a bad moon (St. Comb's).

The new moon lying on her back is likened to a cup to hold water, which is emptied during her course. On the other hand, if the new moon stands well up, it is regarded as a sign of good weather (general).

When the new moon is " sharp i' the corners", the saying is : " She's nae a good moon." When she is blunt and round she is a good moon. There is another saying : " She's ower like a coo's horn to be good" (Rosehearty).

When she appears " stracht (straight) and fair-set" she is looked upon as a good moon (Rosehearty).

If there are heavy clouds about the time of moon-rise the fishermen watch what will follow. If the clouds disperse the weather remains good, but if the clouds remain there is foul weather at hand (Rosehearty).

[1] *D.*, p. 59.
[2] *D.*, p. 61, under " New Moon". *M.*, p. 16 (14).

A circle round the moon is called : A broch (general), meen-bow (Rosehearty, Broadsea), meen-ring, the rim (Nairn), the wheel, and the big wheel (Nairn).

In St. Comb's the expression is : " The bigger the bow, the nearer the weather"; and in Cove, " The bigger the ring, the nearer the breeze".[1]

When there is much of a green colour in the circle it is an indication of rain ; but if its colour is pale, windy weather is at hand (Cairnbulg).

If the inner edge of the circle is pretty bright in green and yellow, it is an indication of rain (Nairn).

Often there is an opening in it.   It indicates the direction from which the wind is to blow (general).

The small halo that appears round the moon, somewhat like a corona goes, by the name of " Cock's Eye" (general) and " Keelan's Ee", *i.e.*, the eye of the small cod-fish.   It is believed to indicate stormy weather.

III.—THE STARS.

When the stars twinkle much, or when they look near, a change of weather is looked for (Rosehearty).

When the stars in a calm, during weather without frost, begin to twinkle—" lamp"—with more brightness, wind is not far distant[2] (Pittulie).

When the stars are reflected very brightly in the pools left by the tide, and twinkle much—" lamp"—during frosty weather, it is regarded as an indication of a change of weather (Pittulie).

When a large star is near the moon stormy weather is looked upon as not far off (general).   It goes by the name of " Madge" in Macduff, and the saying is : " Madge is ower near the meen."

In Portessie the position of the star is taken into account,

[1] *D.*, p. 60, under " Halo", and p. 61, under " Moon Halo".   *M.*, p. 16 (6).

[2] *D.*, p. 73, under " Flickering," and p. 74, under " Twinkling".

whether "afore" or "ahin" the moon. If before the moon, *i.e.*, to the west, stormy weather follows; but if behind or to the east, fair weather; and one speaks of the "ship towin the boat", and the "boat towin the ship".

Shooting stars, "sheetin or fa'in starns", indicate the direction to which the wind will blow (Rosehearty).

IV.—THE RAINBOW.

> "A rainbow in the morning
> Bids the sailor take warning;
> A rainbow at night
> Is the shepherd's delight."

> "A rainbow in the morning,
> Sailors take warning;
> A rainbow at night
> Is the sailor's delight."[1]   (General.)

A piece of a rainbow on the horizon is called Bleerie (Macduff). Bleeze, *i.e.*, blaze (Macduff). Bonnie thing (Macduff). Fire (Buckie). Fiery Ee (Macduff). Fiery teeth, *i.e.*, tooth (Macduff). Giltin (St. Comb's). Rawnie, *i.e.*, small roe (Macduff). Rose (Nairn). Silk-napkin (Crovie). Teeth, *i.e.*, tooth (general).

Robbie Buchan—this name was applied by an old fisherman of Broadsea, near Fraserburgh. He died about fifteen years ago, at the age of eighty. This seems, however, a mere fancy name.

Its appearance is looked upon as forecasting unsettled or "royit" weather, particularly if it is behind the sun (general).

The fishermen of Macduff believe that a breeze will blow in a short time from the quarter in which it appears. Thus they say: "There's a rawn (roe) roastin' i' the nor'-wast; we'll hae a breeze shortly."[2]

If a "rose" appears in the south-east with a flood tide, *i.e.*, a flowing tide, and the wind blowing from south-west,

---

[1] *D.*, p. 71, under "Night and Morning Rainbow". *M.*, p. 16 (8).
[2] *M.*, p. 16 (13).

the wind shortly blows from S.E. If the tide is ebbing the wind will blow from north-west, with rain (Nairn).

V.—THE AURORA BOREALIS.

The Aurora Borealis is called Dancers, Merry Dancers, Northern Lichts—*i.e.*, Lights and Streamers.

If the Aurora appears during spring, some fishermen (Macduff) observe that soon after the wind blows "into it", that is, from the opposite quarter. When it appears in autumn the wind blows from the quarter in which it makes its appearance.[1]

The Aurora is the forerunner of southerly winds (Rose-hearty).

If it remains pretty low on the northern horizon, it indicates no change of weather, but, in the opinion of some, with the wind from the north. If it rises high, and passes "the line", *i.e.*, the zenith (Pittulie), or "the crap o' the air", towards the south-west, stormy weather follows (Pittulie, St. Comb's), with wind from the south according to some.

If the sky is dark below the Aurora, some fishermen assert that southerly winds are at hand.

VI.—LIGHTNING.

Lightning at night without thunder is commonly called "fire flaucht", and is looked upon as the precursor of windy weather (general), "flauchty weather" (Pittulie). About the month of September it indicates a westerly breeze, and within no long time after its appearance. Thus if it appears early in the evening the breeze springs up by morning.[2]

VII.—THUNDER.

Thunder in the forenoon is said to be followed by a breeze from the north or north-east. Thunder in the afternoon is followed by fine warm weather (Rosehearty).

[1] *M.*, p. 16 (9).   [2] *M.*, p. 16 (11).

If the wind blows from the west or north-west, and towards evening goes to the north, it is called the "wife that goes out at even", and soon springs up into a breeze (Macduff).

If the wind blows from the south-west, with blackness in the west and a bank of cloud to the east, the wind backs to the south before the blackness in the west, and rises to a breeze (Pittulie).

XIII.—FROST.

If hoar frost, or "white frost", continues for two days, it commonly ends on the third day with foul weather.

> "Three white frosts all in a row
> Ends either in frost or snow",

is a Kincardineshire rhyme. It is looked upon as a forerunner of a breeze (Rosehearty).

The fishermen have a saying that frost "grips doon, or conquers, the ween and the sea" (general).

XIV.—HILLS.

If distant hills are seen clearly, rain is not far off.

When the hills on the north side of the Moray Firth are seen from the south side in Banff and Aberdeenshire, a change of weather is looked for within a short time (general).

XV.—LIVING CREATURES.

The dog[1] eating grass, and the cat washing its face,[2] are indications of rain not far off (general, inland).

The "louper-dog" (the porpoise) plunging through the sea indicates approaching stormy weather (St. Comb's, Pittulie, etc.). It goes against the wind.

[1] *D.*, pp. 29, 30, 31, under "Cats and Dogs".
[2] *M.*, p. 20 (B.) (4). *Biblioteca de las Tradiciones Españoles*, vol. iv, pp. 87, 89.

When sea-birds fly high stormy weather is not far off (Portessie).

When sea-birds fly high and wheel round and round before the wind, a breeze is not far off. When the breeze comes the birds face it (Macduff).

When sea-birds fly high in circles stormy weather is at hand. When they fly to sea eastward it is a sign of settled weather (St. Comb's).

Birds flying high and wheeling round and round indicate a " changin win" (Pittulie).

If the scratt (cormorant) fly through the wind at night it is an indication of fair weather, but, if the bird fly before it, stormy weather is looked for (Macduff).

When the mawr or queet, in the early morning, utters out at sea the notes ur-r-r-r, " a fine easterly haar is comin up" (Pittulie).

When gulls fly high "in the top of the air" a northerly breeze is not far off (Macduff).

If ducks dart through the pond they are swimming in and flap their wings, it is looked upon as indicating a coming breeze (Keith, inland). When doing so, they are said to be "leukin for ween."[1]

When swallows fly low stormy weather is at hand.[2]

A larger number of midges than ordinary is an indication of rain.

When herring rise and swim in shoals on the surface, which some fishermen (Macduff) call " brushin", the saying is : " The herrin's brushin ; they'll get a gale i' their tail."

When mackerel rise to the surface and rush through the water flapping their tails, a breeze is approaching (Pittulie, Rosehearty).

If salmon are seen leaping in numbers a breeze is approaching (Macduff).

When the "saithe"—the young of the cod-fish—comes to the surface in shoals, a breeze is looked for (Rosehearty).

---

[1] *D.*, p. 40, under " Waterfowl".

[2] *D.*, p. 40, under " Swallow" ; *M.*, p. 20 (7).

APPENDIX.

The Milky Way is called " The White Strip" (Nairn).

John Stro is the name of the " Man in the Moon". He is the Jew that gathered sticks on the Sabbath day in the Wilderness, and was stoned to death (Keith) ; and he is spoken of as "the man wi' the birn o' sticks on 's back".

The three stars of Orion's Belt bear the name of " The Lady's Elvan" (ell-wand) ; and the Hyades that of " The Sawen Starns" (Keith).

Venus, as the Morning Star, is called " The Star of Bethlehem" (Nairn).

WALTER GREGOR.

WEATHER PROVERBS AND SAYINGS

NOT CONTAINED IN

INWARDS' OR SWAINSON'S BOOKS.

BY C. W. EMPSON.

HAVE compared the collections of *Weather Proverbs*, published by Inwards and Swainson with a MS. collection of my own, and the following is a transcript of those which I cannot find in their books. Some of these I sent to Inwards several years ago, placing them at his disposal for a second edition of his book, but a second edition has not apparently been called for.

Figures between square brackets denote old style. I consider it a great omission in Inwards' and Swainson's books that they do not attribute ancient proverbs to days *old* style. Unless you do so you cannot make fair comparisons. I have drawn attention to this in my " Notes on Weather Proverbs " in the *Leisure Hour* for 1876, p. 14. The arrangement of my notes follows that of Inwards's book.

> Oak, smoke,
> Ash, squash.—*Kent.*

> If the oak is out before the ash
> 'Twill be a summer of wet and splash.
> But if the ash is before the oak
> 'Twill be a summer of fire and smoke.

When the Great Bear is on this side of the North Pole, the summer is dry ; if he gets on the other side, the summer is wet, especially if he be then in conjunction with Venus and Jupiter.— *Yorkshire.*

If the ice will bear a man before Christmas, it will not bear a duck after.—*Notts.*

Breast-bone of goose dark-coloured after cooking, no genial spring, and *vice versâ—Lincoln.*

[In Richmondshire for " goose " read " duck " in above.]

6 *Jan.* [18 *Jan.*] At Twelfth Day the days are lengthened a cock's stride.—*Italian.*

Jan. and May. A warm January, a cold May.

2 *Feb.* [14 *Feb.*]—

> If it neither rains nor snows on Candlemas Day,
> You may striddle your horse and go and buy hay.—*Lincoln.*

> Candlemass Day ! Candlemass Day !
> Half our fire, and half our hay.

[*i.e.,* half through winter only, and so half our provisions should be left.]

> You should on Candlemass Day
> Throw candle and candlestick away.

> Snow at Candlemass
> Stops to handle us.—*Rutland.*

March. In March, and at all seasons of the year when the judges are on circuit and there are criminals to be hanged, storms prevail.—*Grantham.*

A peck of March dust is worth an *Earl's* ransom, "when do vall on thornen leaves."—*Dorset.*

March and August.—A wet March makes a sad August.

April. It is always cold when the blackthorn comes into flower.—*Surrey.*

" Blackthorn winter."—*Hants, Kent.*

Whatever the weather may be on Easter Day, such it will be during harvest.—*Yorkshire.*

A late Easter a long cold spring.

> A wet Good Friday and wet Easter Day
> Makes plenty of grass and very little hay.

13 *May.* About this day it is always cold. Professor Erman of Berlin, writing to the astronomer Arago in 1840, says :—" The two swarms or currents of planetary bodies (meteors, &c.) which the earth meets on the ecliptic, respectively about 10th of August and 13th of November, annually interpose themselves between her and the sun, the first during the days comprised between the 5th and 11th of February, the second from the 10th to the 13th of May. Each of these conjunctions causes annually at these periods a very notable extinction of the calorific rays of the sun, and thereby lowers the temperature at all the points of the earth's surface."

Fine on Holy Thursday, wet on Whit-Monday.

Wet on Holy Thursday, fine on Whit-Monday.

July. The first Friday in July is always wet.—*London.*

13 *July* [25 *July*]. Margaret's Flood.

15 *July.* (S. Gallo's Day). The weather on this day will prevail for
.   forty days after.—*Tuscany.*

Or,

To any day within the octave of the Feast of S. Bartholomew.—
Rome.

19 *Sept.* [1 *Oct.*] Storm from south, mild winter.—*Derby.*

21 *Sept.* A quiet week before the autumn equinox and after, the temperature will continue higher than usual into the winter.

S. Matthew sends the sap into the tree.

29 *Sept.* [11 *Oct.*] On Michaelmas Day the devil puts his foot on the blackberries.—*N. Ireland.*

October always has twenty-one fine days.

11 *November* [23 *Nov.*] From whatever quarter the wind blows at midnight at Martinmas Eve, it will continue there mostly for the next three months. N.W. wind bodes a hard winter.—*Notts.*

31 *October* [12 *November*]—

> If ducks do slide at Hollandtide,
> At Christmas they will swim ;
> If ducks do swim at Hollandtide,
> At Christmas they will slide.—*Bucks.*

21 *December*—

> Lucy light ! Lucy light !
> Longest day ard shortest night !

Sun —

> An evening gray and morning red
> Will send the shepherd wet to bed.

A gaudy morning bodes a wet afternoon.

Moon. A Wednesday's change is bad.—*N. Italy.*

A Saturday new moon, if it comes once in seven years, comes too often for sailors.—*Dorset.*

> In the waning of the moon
> A cloudy morn—fair afternoon.
> —*Hone's Year Book*, p. 299.
>
> A fog and a small moon
> Bring an easterly wind soon.—*Cornwall.*

If a big star is dogging the moon, wild weather may be expected. —*Nautical.*

"If a star is seen near the moon, which they (the fishermen) call Hurlbassey, tempestuous weather is looked for by them."— M'Skimin, *History of Carrickfergus* (A.D. 1823).

"One star a-head of the moon towing her, and another astern chasing her," a sure sign of storm.—*Torquay.*

The weather remains the same during the whole moon.

(A.) Eleven times out of twelve, as it is on the fifth day, if it continues unchanged over the sixth day ;

(B.) Nine times out of twelve, as it is on the fourth day, if the sixth day resembles the fourth.

Wind. There are certain weather-holes or wind-holes, *i.e.,* caverns and clefts, which stand to the inhabitants of the Alps instead of barometers. When the wind blows cold from them the weather may be expected fine.—Schenchzer, *Naturgeschichte,* iv. 122.

Similar hole near a gap in the Malvern Hills called " the Wytche. '

We shall have rain, for the wind is in Bodjham Hole.—*Ashford Vale, East Kent.*

WEATHER PROVERBS AND SAYINGS.

There'll be some rain, for the wind has got into Habberley Hole.—
Shrewsbury.

> An out [southerly] wind and a fog
> ring an east wind home snug.—*Cornwall.*

Clouds—

> If Bever hath a cap,
> Ye churles of the Vale, look to that.—*Leicestershire.*

> When Hood Hill has on its cap,
> Hamilton's sure to come down with a clap.—*Cleveland.*[*]

> When Eston nabbe puts on a cloake,
>   And Roysberrye a cappe,
> Then all the folks on Clevelands clay
>   Ken there will be a clappe.—*Yorkshire.*

> When Roseberry Topping wears a hat
> Morden Carre will suffer for that.—*Yorkshire.*

> When Oliver's Mount puts on his hat
> Scarborough town will pay for that.—*Yorkshire.*

> When Percelly weareth a hat
> All Pembrokeshire shall weet of that.—*Pembroke.*

> When Ladie Lift
> Puts on her shift,
> She feares a downright raine ;
>   But when she doffs it, you will finde
>   The raine is o'er, and still the winde,
> And Phœbus shine againe.—*Herefordshire.*
> [Lady Lift Clump is a clump of trees near Weobley.]

> When the clouds go up the hill
> They'll send down water to turn a mill.

> When Tottenham Wood is all a fire
> Then Tottenham Street is nought but mire.—*Middlesex.*

" Spreading the table-cloth," on Table Mountain.—*Cape of Good
Hope.*

Rain. Wet continues if the ground dries up too soon.

When rain threatens in the morning it is likely to rain when the
sun and the wind get together.

> Rain afore church,
> Rain all the week, little or much.—*Norfolk.*

[* For this and the three following rhymes see *ante*, vol. i. pp. 160–175.—*Ed.*]

If in handling bread you break it into two parts it will rain for a whole week.

Rainbow—Rainbow in the south brings heavy rain ; in the west, slight showers and dew ; in the east, fair weather.

A Saturday's rainbow is sure to be followed by a week of rotten (rainy) weather.—*S. Ireland.*

Thunder—

> If it sinks from the north
> It will double its wrath.
> If it sinks from the south
> It will open its mouth.
> If it sinks from the west
> It is never at rest.
> If it sinks from the east
> It will leave us at peace.—*Kent.*

Frost. Three white frosts bring rain.

Hoar frost and gypsies never stay nine days in a place.

Cattle. On a wet day, if cattle are all lying down in the fields it will clear up ; but the reverse if they stand about.—*Wilts.*

If cattle remain on the top of the hills it will be fine ; but wet if they descend to the valleys.—*Derbyshire.*

Moles. If during frost moles throw up fresh earth the frost will disappear in forty-eight hours.

Previously to the setting in of winter the mole prepares a sort of basin, forming it in a bed of clay, which will hold about a quart. In this basin a great quantity of worms are deposited, and in order to prevent their escape they are partly mutilated but not so as to kill them. On these worms the mole feeds in winter. When these basins are few in number the following winter will be mild.—*Cottage Gardener*, i. 73 (Nov. 1848).

Birds. It is said that the flight of wild geese is always in the form either of letters or of figures, and that the figure denotes the number of weeks of frost that will follow their appearance.

If birds begin to whistle in the early morning in winter it bodes frost.

The often doping or diving of waterfowl foreshows rain is at hand.
—*Shepherd's Calendar.*

Frogs. If bright yellow frogs are to be seen now and then it is a good sign of a fine harvest.—*Derbyshire.*

If frogs are very active in jumping, rain is not far off.

Snakes. Fresh tracks of snakes bode rain if they are numerous.—*Italy.*

Plants—

> When elm leaves are as big as a shilling,
> Plant kidney beans, if to plant'em you're willing.
> When elm leaves are as big as a penny,
> You *must* plant kidney beans if you mean to have any.

> When the elmen leaf is as big as a mouse's ear,
> Then to sow barley never fear.
> When the elmen leaf is as big as an ox's eye,
> Then says, " Hie ! boys ! hie ! "

Stone. The sweating of tombs or stone pillars denotes rain.—*Shepherd's Calendar.*

Wheat. Abundant wheat crops never follow a mild winter.

SUPERSTITIONS OF THE SCOTTISH FISHERMEN.

IN "The Pirate" Sir Walter Scott introduces us to the old Norse belief—a belief still held, we are told, by some of our northern fishing communities—that whoever saves a drowning man must reckon on him ever after as an enemy. This has often been remarked by fishermen as a strangely-mysterious fact. Also, that when the crew of some boat or vessel have perished with but the exception of one individual, the relatives of the deceased invariably regard that one with a deep, irrepressible hatred. In both cases these feelings, engendered of hostility and dislike, are said not simply to arise from grief, envy, or a burdensome gratitude, but in some "occult and supernatural cause." The following singular occurence strikingly illustrates the case in point. About the beginning of last century a Cromarty boat was wrecked on the wild shores of Eathie. All the crew perished with the exception of one fisherman, who, sad to relate, was so persecuted on account of his good fortune by the relatives of the drowned men, who even threatened his life, that he was obliged, sorely against his inclination, to leave his native Cromarty and seek refuge at Nairn. Not many years afterwards he had the misfortune to be wrecked a second time, and again he chanced to be the sole survivor. As on the former occasion, he was subjected to such persistent persecution on the part of the friends of the deceased that he was compelled to quit Nairn, for what harbour of refuge is not recorded.

There is a church in Fladda dedicated to St. Columba. It has an altar in the west end, and on it a blue stone of round form, which is always moist. It was an ordinary custom when any of the fishermen were detained in the island by contrary winds to wash this blue stone with water, in the hope of procuring a favouring breeze. This practice was said never to fail, especially if a stranger washed the stone.

Until within recent years no Cockenzie fisherman would have ventured out to sea had either a pig or a lame man crossed his path on his way to the beach. Not only so, but had a stranger met him of a morning and been the first to greet him with "*a gude mornin*" he would have regarded the interruption as an evil omen, and remained at home that day at least.

Another curious and superstitious custom used to prevail amongst fishermen. If, when at sea, especially when going out or coming into port, any one was heard to take the name of God in vain the first to hear the expression immediately called out " Cauld airn," when each of the boat's crew would instantly grasp fast the first piece of iron which came within his reach, and hold it for a time between his hands. This was done by way of counteracting the ill-luck which otherwise would have continued to follow the boat for the remainder of the day.

The ancient bell which formerly rung the good people of St. Manance to church, being suspended from a tree in the church-yard, was, strange to say, removed every year from that position during the herring season, the fishermen entertaining the super-stitious belief that the fish were scared away from the coast by its noise !

Before striking their tents at Lammas, and bidding farewell for a while to the active, perilous occupations of the summer, the Orkney fishermen, who had been accustomed to associate during the season, met and partook of a parting cup, when the usual toast was, " Lord, open Thou the mouth of the grey fish and hold Thy hand above the corn !" This meeting was known by the name of the " Fishers' Foy."

From time immemorial the fishermen and seamen of Burghead, in Duffus parish, Elginshire, on Yule Night, o. s., met at the west end of the town, carrying an old barrel and other combustible materials, of which the following additional note may be recorded—

This barrel having been sawn in two, the lower half is nailed into a long spoke of firewood, which serves for a handle. *This nail must not be struck by a hammer*, but driven in by a stone. The half-barrel is then filled with dry wood saturated with tar, and built up like a pyramid, leaving only a hollow to receive a burning peat, *for no lucifer-match must be applied.* Should the bearer stumble or fall the consequences would be unlucky to the town and to himself. The Clavie is thrown down the western side of the hill, and a desperate scramble ensues for the burning brands, possession of which is accounted to bring good luck, and the embers are carried home and carefully preserved till the following year as a safeguard against all manner of evil. In bygone times it was thought necessary that one man should carry it right round the town, so the strongest was selected for the purpose. It was also customary to carry the Clavie round every ship in the harbour, a part of the ceremony which has lately been discontinued. In 1875, however, the Clavie was duly carried to one vessel just ready for sea. Handfuls of grain were thrown upon her deck, and amid a shower of fire-water she received the suggestive name of "Doorie." The modern part of the town is not included in the circuit. According to a correspondent of *Notes and Queries*, ser. I. vol. v. p. 5, the following superstitious observances formerly existed among the fishermen of Preston Pans :

If on their way to their boats they met a pig they at once turned back, and deferred their embarkation. The event was an omen that boded ill to their fishing.

It was a custom also of theirs to set out on the Sunday for the fishing grounds. A clergyman of the town was said to pray against their Sabbath-breaking, and to prevent any injury which might result from his prayers, the fishermen made a small image of rags and burned it on the tops of their chimneys.

In the year 1885 some of the fishermen of Buckie, owing to the herring fishing being very backward, dressed a cooper in a flannel shirt with burs stuck all over it; and in this condition he was carried in procession through the town in a hand-barrow. This was done to bring better luck to the fishing.

There were formerly fishermen in Forfarshire, who, on a hare crossing their path while on their way to their boats, would not put to sea that day.

In some parts of Scotland, when a horseshoe that has been found is nailed to the mast of a fishing-boat, it is supposed to ensure the boat's safety in a storm.

A practice common among the Cromarty fishermen of the last age was termed " soothing the waves." When beating up in stormy weather along a lee shore, it was customary for one of the men to take his place on the weather gunwale, and there continue waving his hand in a direction opposite to the sweep of the sea, in the belief that this species of appeal to it would induce it to lessen its force. It was also (perhaps still is) customary with fishermen and seafaring men, when the sails were drooping against the mast, and the vessel lagging in her course, earnestly to invoke the wind in a shrill trembling whistle, with their faces turned in the direction whence they expect the breeze, pausing when a slight increase of air made itself felt, and renewing their solicitations yet more earnestly when it had died away.   ELLEN E. GUTHRIE.

SOME FOLK-LORE OF THE SEA.

By the Rev. Walter Gregor.

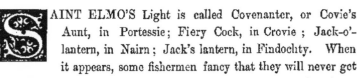

AINT ELMO'S Light is called Covenanter, or Covie's Aunt, in Portessie; Fiery Cock, in Crovie ; Jack-o'-lantern, in Nairn ; Jack's lantern, in Findochty. When it appears, some fishermen fancy that they will never get to land, or that some disaster will fall upon them. (Portessie).   Some think that the death of one of the relatives of the crew is not far off, and that the light is the ghost or spirit.[*] (Nairn.)

The phosphorescence of the sea goes in Nairn by the names of " burnin wattir " and " fiery wattir."[†]

When it begins to appear on the sea, a Nairn fisherman would say: " The sea's firin "; and when at the herring-fishing, before casting the nets, " Wait till the wattir fires."

The dulness that appears in the sea during the month of May is spoken of as " the easterly wattir "; and the fishermen say, " The sea's alive wi' the livin breed," or, " The sea's alive wi' the livin vermin." [‡] (Crovie.)

The Storm.

In Buckie and the neighbouring villages the sound of the sea coming from the west bears the name of " the chant fae (from) the saans (sands) o' Spey," and is regarded as a token of good weather. The Nairn folks call this wind from the west " the sooch (ch guttural) o' the sea," and regard it as a forecast of fine weather.[§]

---

[*] Δημωδεις μετεωρολογικοι Μυθοι, by N. G. Polites, p. 14.
[†] Folk-Lore Journal, vol. iii. pp. 53, 306.
[‡] Ibid. vol. iii. p. 306.
[§] Ibid. vol. iii. p. 54.

At Portessie and along the shore of the Moray Firth, on the Banff and Morayshire coasts, before a storm from the north or north-east, the sea becomes perfectly calm, "like a beuk (book) leaf," as my informant expressed it, and the phenomenon is called a "weather gaa."

The swell before the storm is called "the win-chap."* (Portessie.) The broken water on the shore goes by the name of "the breach." (Nairn.) When the waves are heavy at the mouth of the harbour (Nairn), so that the boats cannot go to sea, the fishermen say, "There's ower muckle sea-gate."

The fisher folks of Portessie say that the sea before any disaster of drowning has "a waichty (weighty) melody," "a dead groan," or simply "a groan." In Nairn they speak of "a waichty groan" before any fatality takes place.†

In Portessie and Buckie the belief exists that the sea cannot become calm till the body of the drowned that is destined to be buried has been found ;—in the words of my informant, "gehn (if) the body is t' get cirsent meels (consecrated ground), the sea's never at rist (rest) till the body's ashore."

Said a Portessie fisherman : " We were going to Beauly with fish and oil. The wind came down strong against us, and we had to go into Burghead. We lay there for two days, with the wind always a-head. There was a queer woman in Forres, and we did not know whether the woman, in whose house we were, sent for her or not, but she came into the house. She asked us what we were doing here. We told her. She said we would be in Beauly in two hours. We went out, and, though the wind was against us when the woman came in, found it had changed in our favour. We put out at once, and in two hours we were in Beauly."

" We were in Potmahomack once. A woman there baked a bannock, and gave it to one of the crew, with strict orders not to break it till he reached home, in order to get a 'roon win'.' The bannock was carefully rolled in a napkin, and put into his breast. In

---

* *Folk-Lore Journal*, vol. iii. pp. 53, 305.
† *Ibid*. vol. iii. pp. 53, 54, 306.

climbing up a rope into the boat—'breestin' the boat'—the bannock
was broken. The wind was quite favourable when the boat set sail,
but in a short time a heavy breeze came down, and home was reached
after the greatest difficulty."

"On another occasion," said he, "we got a piece of twine with
three knots upon it. One knot was to be loosed when the sail was
hoisted. The second was to be loosed after a time to freshen the
wind. All went well for a time, but after a little it fell 'breath-
calm.' The third knot was loosed, but hardly was this done when a
storm burst upon us, and we hardly escaped with the life."

A fisherman of Banff was at one time in Invergordon. When
there, he showed some kindness to a woman by giving her fish. When
the boat was about to return, the woman presented herself, and gave
the fishermen a bottle with strict orders not to uncork it till they
reached harbour at home. Curiosity, however, overcame all fears,
and the boat had not half accomplished the voyage when the bottle
was unstopped. In the course of a short time a breeze burst upon
the boat, and it was with the utmost difficulty land was reached.
(Told by J. R., Rosehearty.)

The Tide.

When the tide is running on the parts of the sea between the
shallows and the deeps there is commonly a good deal of swell, and,
if the weather is in the least rough, great care must be taken in
passing through this swell. It is called "the tripple o' tide."
(Pittulie.)

When the tide is lowest it is called "slack tide" (Findochty), and
the point of time is called "the slack o' the tide."

At Portessie the fisher folks do not begin any piece of work, such
as barking nets, baiting lines, &c., except when the tide is "flouwin."
As my informant said to me, "I pit on the barkin pan fin the tide
begins t' flouw." *

Hens must be set when the tide is flowing. The chickens are
stronger, and thrive better. (Buckie.)

* *Folk-Lore Journal*, vol. ii. p. 356.

In parts of the West Highlands the fisher folks build rough stone dykes across the mouths of the small inlets, so as to form convenient places for keeping crabs and lobsters alive. My informant said he has often seated himself on a dyke and watched the conduct of the prisoners, and the moment the water of the rising tide entered through the stones they were in motion to meet it.

Here is a theory of the movements of the herring. When the tide begins to rise, the herrings that were lying at the bottom rise, and are carried southward with the flowing tide. When the tide begins to ebb, the herrings again go to the bottom, and lie till the tide begins to flow, when they again rise, and are carried farther southward. This accounts for the southern migration of the herring. (Findochty.)

The Boat.

Some boats are supposed to be unlucky, "have an unlucky spehl in them." I heard of a carpenter, now dead, that pretended to forecast what the fortune of the boat would be by the way a certain "spehl," or chip of wood, came off when he began the work of building.

Fishermen (Nairn) speak of "he-wood" and "she-wood," and they say that a boat built of "she-wood" sails faster during night than during day. They believe that one built of "stealt" (stolen) wood does the same. "A thief goes fast at night," said my informant.

To secure luck in fishing, the owner's wife must, when the boat is tarred, put on the first mop of tar. (Porthnockie.)

The boat has always to be turned, when in harbour, according to the course of the sun. The phrase in Buckie is: "Pit the boat's head wast aboot" (west about).*

When a new boat was to be brought home (Crovie), those, that were to do so, set out when the tide was "flouwin." When the boat arrived, the village turned out to meet her, and bread and cheese, with beer or whiskey, were given to all. A glass, with spirits or beer, was broken on the boat, and a wish for success was expressed in such form

* _Folk-Lore of the North-East of Scotland_, p. 199.

as : "I wiss (wish) this ane may gyang (go) as lang safe oot and in, an catch as mony fish as the aul' ane."

It is accounted unlucky to go for a new boat, and come back without her. J. Watt, of Crovie, went to Pennan for a new boat. She was not finished, and he had to return empty-handed. He went for her some time after, and brought her home on Saturday. On Monday, Tuesday, and Wednesday, he proceeded to the fishing, and everything went right. But there was something that had to be remedied about the sail. The boat had to be taken to Macduff for this purpose. On Friday the journey was undertaken. When off Gamrie Mohr, a high headland, a gust of wind came down, and sank the boat. One man was drowned. The boat was afterwards recovered, but she had to be sold, as the crew would not go to sea in her. She proved a good seaworthy craft. The gusts off this headland go by the name of the "flans o' Mohr," and are accounted more dangerous than the gusts or "flans" off the other headlands. (Flan, a gust of wind from above.)

When the new boat was brought home (Portessie), the fisher folks assembled beside the boat. One of them "flang bere in ower the boat, sang oot the boat's name, and three cheers wiz geen (given)." Then followed the "boat fehst" (feast)—bread, cheese, whiskey, or porter, or a dinner of broth, beef, &c., accompanied with quantities of whiskey. At this feast attended often all the men of the village, if small, and each set of men sat together. In each of the large fishing boats there are eight men besides the skipper. Each man has his own seat in rowing, and always keeps it. Counting from the stem, the first man on the left is called "the aivran hank," or "hanksman," whilst his companion on the right is called "the farran hank," or "hanksman." The second two go by the names of "the aivran mid-ship" and "the farran mid-ship." The third pair has the names of "the aivran slip" and "the farran slip"; and the fourth, those of "the aivran boo" and "the farran boo." The master is "the skipper." At the feast all the skippers sat together, all the "aivran hanksmen," or "aivran hanks," sat together, and so on with the others. The drinking was often carried far into the night, and even into the morning. A common toast was, "I wis you may burn 'er."

A toast, frequently used at feasts and drinking bouts, was:

> " Health t' men, an death t' fish,
> They're waggin their tails, it'll pay for this."

The Line.

When a new line was to be made by a few neighbours, it had to be begun when the tide was rising, and finished without any interruption, so that all might have a share in the "allooance," that is, the whiskey that was drunk for luck, on completion of the work. (Crovie.)

In Portessie, Buckie, and other villages, the first one that enters the house when a "greatlin"—a great line, that is, a line for catching cod, ling, skate, and the larger kinds of fish—is being made, has to pay for a mutchkin of whiskey, which is drunk in the house after the line is finished. "The line gets the first glass," that is, the first glassful is poured over the line.

A story is current that an old fisherman, who was somewhat fond of "a dram," had very often a new great line—"ane in the month," ths explanation of which was, that he kept one by him, and, when he was anxious for a glass, he took out his new line, so that, when a neighbour came in, he was busy measuring it off, and working at it. His "teename" was Old Pro.*

The first hook baited is spit upon, and then laid in the scull. My informant told me that she invariably followed this practice. She also told me that it is a custom to spit in the fire when the "girdle" is taken off the fire when the baking of the bread, oaten cakes, is finished.

The Good and the Ill Fit, &c.

If one with an "ill fit" was met when going to the boat to proceed to sea, there were some that would not have gone till the next tide had flowed. (Buckie.)

There were some that, if they had met one who asked them on their way to the sea where they were going, would have struck the one so

* *Folk-Lore Journal*, vol. iii. p. 307.

asking "to draw blood," and thus turn away the ill luck that was believed (Portessie) to follow such a question.

A person with flat-soled feet is looked upon as an "unlucky fit." (Nairn.)

It is a notion among some that if you see below one having an "ill fit," no harm will follow. One morning a Spey salmon-fisher said to his companion on meeting him to proceed to their work, that he had met a certain man well known as having an "ill fit." "We'll hae naething the day, than." "Oh, bit he wiz ridin, an I saw through aneth (below) the horse-belly," was the answer.

Another mode of counteracting the evil of an "ill fit" is to have "the first word o' the one that has the evil power," that is, to be the first to speak. An old woman of the name of P—— lived in Fraserburg. She had the repute of having an "ill fit," and fishermen did not like to meet her. She kept a cow or two, and pastured them along the sides of the public roads, and no one that passed along the roads ever could have "the first word on her." She made it a point of being the first to speak. (Told by a Pittulie fisherman.)

As some people are looked upon as having an "ill fit," others are regarded as carrying luck with them. Such as have led an immoral life, whether man or woman, are those that bring success, and the name of such a one is used as a talisman. Thus (Buckie) when beginning to shoot the lines one of the crew will say, "We'll try in ——'s name for luck." When the line, on being hauled, sticks on the bottom, it is said, "Up, or rise ——." Sometime ago, the name of Maggie Bowie, an old woman, was frequently used. (Portessie.) In Buckie a talisman was "Nelltock," the familiar name of a well-known woman, and the saying was, "Blow up, Nelltock."

The cat, the rat, the hare, and the salmon are all bringers of ill-luck, and the words were never uttered during the time the lines were being baited. (Crovie.)

To meet the cat in the morning as the "first fit" was the sure fore-runner of disaster that day.

A. R——, of Crovie, did not leave his bed in the morning without calling out "Hish, hish, hish," to drive away the house cat, lest it might be lying near, and thus be his "first fit."

A fisherman will not keep a pig for feeding (Buckie), and the word pig or swine, as well as rottin (rot), salmon, which is commonly called "the fool (foul) beest," hare, and rabbit, are words of ill-omen. (Buckie.)*

It is unlucky to catch a sea-gull ("a goo") when out fishing, and keep it on board. My informant told me that one day he caught a gull, with the intention of bringing it ashore to his boy. One of the old men in the boat, in very strong language, ordered him to set it adrift, which was done at once. (Portessie.)

W. W. of Crovie, had gone to the West Highlands to prosecute the cod and ling fishing. The first time the boat went to the fishing-ground the first fish that came up on the line was a ling. The skipper at once ordered it to be thrown overboard, as being unlucky to have a ling for the first fish caught.

The "scull," which holds the lines, must not be overturned in the boat after they have been shot. It is unlucky to do so. (Crovie.) A poor "shot" (catch) of fish is supposed to follow. (Nairn.) It is accounted unlucky to put the foot by accident into the scull ("the scoo") after the lines have been thrown. (Nairn.)

It is unlucky to have a rat on board a boat unless it is caught, and killed. The drawing of blood counteracts the bad luck. (Buckie.)

During the herring-fishing of 1885 a rat appeared in the boat of a Crovie fisherman fishing in Rosehearty. A hunt for the animal was made, and it was caught. The fisherman mentioned the fact on returning to his house, when one of the women said, "Ye'll be sure o' a boat fu' the first time ye gyang oot." Another said, "That's az gueede's (as good's) three hunner (300) cran."

Two Crovie boats were, one spring not long ago, fishing in S. Uist. In the boat of one was caught a rat. The skipper of the other boat made the remark, "This winna (will not) be a rich year fahtever (whatever), for we hinna gotten a beastie."

THE HERRING FISHING.

In Portessie and other neighbouring villages white stones are

---

rejected both as ballast and as lug-stones for the herring-nets ; but in Portessie a " boret-stone," that is a stone bored by the *pholas*, is looked upon as particularly lucky for ballast.*

. It is accounted very unlucky to take a stone of the ballast from another man's boat, and, if one did so, he would be resisted. Neither would one allow a "waicht" (weight) of a herring-net to be taken away. These weights, used for sinking the nets, are small stones tied to the lower side of the net. A man had to cross his neighbour's boat to reach his own. In doing so he lifted a weight to use as a hammer to drive a nail in a part of his own boat. He intended to restore the stone ; but the owner, in very surly fashion, ordered him at once to lay it down. The luck of the fishing was supposed to go with the stone. (Nairn.)

Some will not give away a " fry o' herrin," that is, a few herrings as a dish. The luck of the fishing goes with them. (Nairn.)

If one of the crew makes his water over the boat's side before casting the nets, the boat would have been brought back at once without the nets having been shot. (Porthnockie.)

When the herring fishing was going on in a poor way, in the words of the fisherman that told me—"Fin we wiz jist driven t' desperation," he would say, " Wife, for God's sake, turn your sark ! " (Portessie.)

Another mode to get herring is to put the boat through the " main riggan." My informant said that a friend of his told him he once tried this " fret," and lost his "main riggan."

Another mode of securing herring is the following :—The " tail bow " (buoy)—that is, the buoy fixed to the net thrown first overboard, and, therefore, the farthest from the boat when the whole of the nets—" the fleet "—are overboard,—is cut off in the name of some one reputed as carrying luck. For example, a fisherman of Portessie would say, before beginning to cast the nets, " Cut aff the tail bow in Meggie Bowie's name," to bring the fish into the nets.

J. Watt was engaged in the herring fishing at Gardenston. He was not at all successful, and for over a week had caught nothing

* *Folk-Lore Journal*, vol. iii. p. 308.

One evening as he was proceeding to sea "raither hingen-heedit" (with hanging head), the woman in whose house he was lodging, without saying a word to him, threw the beesom (the broom) after him. That night a good fishing was made. J. Watt told one of the crew (a hired man) what had been done. His remark was : "That's fat (what) did it. Tell 'er t' dee 't (do it) again. (Crovie.)

The same custom holds round the coast.

Another custom to secure a fishing, if it is poor during the herring season, is to throw a handful of salt after the skipper, or any of the crew, as he is leaving the house, or to throw salt over the boat. (Portessie.)

The Haddock, &c.

The black spots on the shoulders of the haddock are called Peter's spots, and it is believed by some fishermen (Crovie) that no one can grasp and hold the fish in the same way. My informant told me he had often tried to do so, and seen others do the same, but to no purpose. The fish slipped from the fingers.

Here are two variants of the haddock rhyme :—

> "Roast me weel, an boil me weel,
> Bit dinna burn ma beens,
> Than ye'll never wint me aboot yir hearth-steens."

And—

> "Roast me an boil me weel,
> An dinna burn ma beens,
> An a'll come t' yir fireside aftner nor eens (once)."* (Portessie.)

Here follows something of a contest between the herring and the flounder or fleuk:—

The herrin' said she wiz the king o' the sea, but the fleuk turnt her moo, an' said she wis 't.

And—

> "She thrawd her moo, says she,
> Faht (what) am I tee,
> Fin (when) the herrin's the king o' the sea ? " (Portessie.)

---

* *Folk-Lore Journal*, vol. iii. pp. 188, 310.

SOME FOLK-LORE OF THE SEA.

It is believed that there is a " beest i' the sea for ilky beest o' the
laan " (land), said a Portessie man to me.*

It was a custom to go to the sea, and draw a pailful of water, and
take it along with a little seaweed to the house on the morning of
New Year's Day. (Portessie.)

Dog Stories.

A fisherman in Crovie had a collie dog. He was always at hand
when the boats were putting to sea. One morning when the men
were on the beach making ready to go to the fishing, the dog got into
a great state of excitement, rushed about, and laid hold of the men
when putting the lines into the boats. His conduct was such, that
the men did not go to sea. Scarcely had they got their lines back to
their houses, than a great storm suddenly burst over the Firth.
Several boats were lost from the other villages.

On another occasion, the owner of the dog was going with his boat
to the south to sell his dried cod and ling. The dog was to be taken
along with him. The boat was to sail from Gardenstone, another
village about a mile distant. It was with the utmost difficulty the
dog could be induced to follow his master. But no sooner did he
reach the boat, than he bolted, and ran back, rushed into the house,
and hid under one of the beds. He was taken by force from his
hiding-place, and carried to the boat. The voyage was performed,
and the boat was returning, and had come as far north as Stone-
haven, when a heavy storm came down, the boat was driven ashore in
the early morning, and two of the crew perished. The third one
escaped through the intervention of the dog. He had become en-
tangled about the wreck, and could not free himself. The dog ran
to the town, went up to the first man he met, began barking and
pulling at him in such a way as to arouse his attention. Off the
dog went. The man followed, and soon saw what had happened.
The fisherman was rescued. This took place many years ago, but the
dog still lives in the memory of the fisher folks.

* *Folk-Lore Journal*, vol. iii. p. 183.

SOME FOLK-LORE OF THE SEA.

AMES given to the sea are :—
  The Haddock Peel (Pool);
  The Herring Peel;
  The Herring Pond.

 " To send one across the Haddock Peel " means to banish one.—
(Keith.)

---

 * In this paper I have used as my authorities Ritson's edition of the *Robin Hood Ballads* and his *Prolegomena* thereto. The latter are chiefly remarkable for an entire absence of the critical faculty.

FISHERMEN'S FOLK-LORE.

1.—Some Marriage Customs of the Fisher-folk of Rosehearty, Pitsligo, Aberdeenshire.

NE part of a bride's "plinisan" is a trunk, "the kist." When her property is to be taken to her future home this trunk is the first article taken from her father's house, and it is often sent unlocked. If it is locked it must be locked after being taken outside. The usual way of removing it is to carry it out, and, without letting it touch the ground, place it in the cart that is to convey it to the bride's own house, and then lock it, if it is to be locked. This custom of not locking inside the house a trunk that is to be taken away is carried out in the case of those who are leaving home to prosecute the fishing at other fishing stations. The trunks of the men and women are packed inside, then carried out, and locked.

The bride should not bake the bridal bread—the oatmeal cakes, neither ought she to do any errands, *i. e.* do any kind of shopping or go messages of any sort.

When the bride is dressed for the marriage she used to set out, and wait upon those whom she had called to the marriage, and tell them to make ready. In doing so she must on no account hold her dress in her hand, and, however wet the weather, she must not tuck it up. J—— R——'s marriage-day was a day of rain. Before setting out to give her friends their call to the marriage, she tucked up her dress. She entered the house of Widow R——. The good widow was amazed, at once took the bride outside, unloosed the tucking-up of her dress and let it fall.

When the bride set out to meet the bridegroom at the hall, or house, or church, in which the ceremony was to take place, great attention was, and still is, paid to the "first fit." A horse is looked upon as particularly lucky, hence the saying, " a hairy fit's a happy fit." The man or woman the bride first met had to give her a silver coin, and she made the person turn, and walk a short distance with her.

The bridal-dress must on no account be changed between the time of marriage and the time for retiring to bed.

The bridal-bed was, and is, usually made up by a woman " having milk in her breasts," helped by one that is looked upon as having a " guid fit " or " a lucky han'." The custom varies.

It is regarded as very unlucky if there is a burial in the village on the day of a marriage.

Sometimes the white bridal-petticoat was made into a dress for the first-born child. The bridal chemise and stockings were laid up to be put on at death.

The first clothes of the first-born were all given away to the nearest of kin for her first-born, beginning with a sister if she required them. So the clothes went from one to another, till they were worn out.

The mother had to go to church before she entered a neighbour's house.

I have been told by one that she has seen a mother, who went into a neighbour's house before going to church, put out.

Something borrowed must be put on the child at the time of baptism, often a shawl to roll the infant in. My informant says that she has given the loan of a shawl in accordance with this "fret." The baptismal dress of the first-born was kept for the eldest daughter's first-born.

2.—THE SEA IN ITS HEALTH-GIVING VIRTUES.

The sea is thought to have great health-giving powers, both in its air and waters. It is supposed to be most efficacious in cases of general debility, indigestion, weakness of the spine and limbs, inflammation of the joints, contraction of the sinews, and rheumatism. Many from the inland, visit during the summer months certain of the sea-coast villages, some merely to breathe the air, others to enjoy bathing as well as to breathe the air. The air is believed to have most effect when the stomach is empty in the morning, and the health-seekers are early astir, and along the shore " to snuff the caller air." *

It was quite common, not many years ago, to use the water as a purgative. When the water was to be put to this purpose, it had to be drunk in the morning before taking any food. As large a draught as possible was drunk. This was followed by another of chalybeate water, if a spring of such was at hand, and, if such was not to be had, by one of spring water. A little " dulse " (*Rhodymenia palmata*) was eaten, and a walk taken. The effect was quick and wonderful, as those who have undergone the ordeal have assured me.

Bathing is most commonly done when the tide is "flouin'" (rising), from the belief that the water is strongest and has most effect at that time. Bathing, when the tide is at its lowest, or even when ebbing, is believed by some to be injurious to health, and a mother of a large family now well-stricken in years in Rosehearty told me that she laid strict orders on her boys never to bathe except in a "flouin'" tide.† It was thought to be safer to take the water head first with a dive, when the depth of water allowed, than to walk slowly into the water, as such an act caused the blood to flow too quickly to the head. If one had not the courage to dive, or if the water was too shallow for that purpose, it was considered wise to drench the head—at least to lave the forehead—before entering the water. When the bather left the water, he ran a distance along the beach, if the nature of it allowed him. Bathers often carried along with them a piece of oaten-cakes—" the chatterin piece," "the shiverin piece"—which they ate during the time they were dressing. The early part of the day was regarded as the best time for bathing; and to bathe with a full stomach, or in a state of perspiration, was looked on as full of danger to health.

* Paul Sébillot, *L'Eau de Mer dans les Superstitions et les Croyances ~opulaires*, p. 6. ("L'Homme," 1884, No. 13, 10 Juillet.)
† In Basse Bretagne the contrary opinion prevails. *Ibid.* p. 6.

With some (Macduff, Rosehearty), at least not many years ago, it was a custom to throw into the water before entering it three stones of different sizes, beginning with the largest. White stones, if they could be found, were preferred (Rosehearty). Others again threw in a few without regard to number. Words were repeated, as the stones were being pitched in, but my informants (Macduff, Rosehearty) could not recall them.*

Bathing in the sea is believed to be much more wholesome than in fresh water. Frequent bathing in fresh water, especially if done oftener than once a day, is looked upon as injurious to health.

Sea-water is much used as a lotion in cases of local inflammation, weakness or stiffness of a joint, and spine disease. The water must be drawn when the tide is "flouin," otherwise it is useless. If it is drawn during the waxing moon, so much the more powerful are its virtues. It is warmed, and the affected part is rubbed downwards as strongly as the patient is able to bear, generally in the morning and evening.

By some the same water is used again and again, from the belief that the oftener it is used the stronger grow its curative powers.

This health-giving power of the rising tide is not confined to human beings. Lugworms (*Arenicola piscatorum, Lamk.*) are much used as bait for fish. When they are not wanted immediately they must be kept alive. It is believed that this can be done only by keeping them among water drawn when the tide is rising. If the water is changed daily they may be preserved alive for eight days or more, whereas, if they are put into water taken from an ebbing or "back-gain" tide, they die within a short time.—(Told by two fishermen of Rosehearty.)

A sea-voyage is supposed to bring about a cure of any lingering disease, such as that arising from indigestion or the liver. Or if a voyage cannot be taken, a sail for a day or a few hours with a "guid twist o' sea-sickness and a guid clean-oot" works wonders. Sea-sickness is commonly believed to be healthful.

It is a common idea that a drenching with sea-water is followed by no such evil consequences as arise from a drenching with fresh

* J. Leite de Vasconcellos, *Tradicoes populares de Portugal*, pp. 69, 70.

water; and one is always told that were the effects in the one case as dangerous as in the other, fishermen and sailors could not live.*

Such are, or have been, some of the beliefs about the sea among the folk of the north-east of Scotland with respect to its health-giving powers. WALTER GREGOR.

Lightning Source UK Ltd.
Milton Keynes UK
UKHW040618150719
346184UK00001B/38/P